FOREWORD

The great South American composer Heitor Villa-Lobos was the first composer from Brazil to achieve truly world-wide fame. This is especially interesting in that he did not accomplish this recognition by joining traditionally oriented music-making circles but, instead, followed his heart by basing so much of his writing on melodies and subjects from his native land. He was known as a pianist and teacher of music, but was himself primarily self-taught. He seemed particularly intrigued by the world of childhood, and many children's folksongs occur in his writing as well as pieces descriptive of children's activities. Villa-Lobos was born in Rio de Janeiro in 1887 and passed on in that city in 1959.

The short but brilliant *O Polichinelo* has a facinating concert history in our own day. It has become a popular encore for some of our finest pianists. Arthur Rubinstein, for example, often played this work as one of his final encores. The piece can be performed so quickly as to seem almost a blur, and this appears not to detract from its musical effectiveness. It is an excerpt from the composer's first *Prole do Bêbê* suite. It sometimes appears on programs listed as *Polichinelle* (the French term); the title refers to a traditional puppet (Punch) that is full of zany antics. The first *Prole do Bêbê* suite contains pieces descriptive of a baby's dolls.

O POLICHINELO
from Prole do Bêbê, No. 1

Heitor Villa-Lobos

* Pedal is often used lightly in these passages.

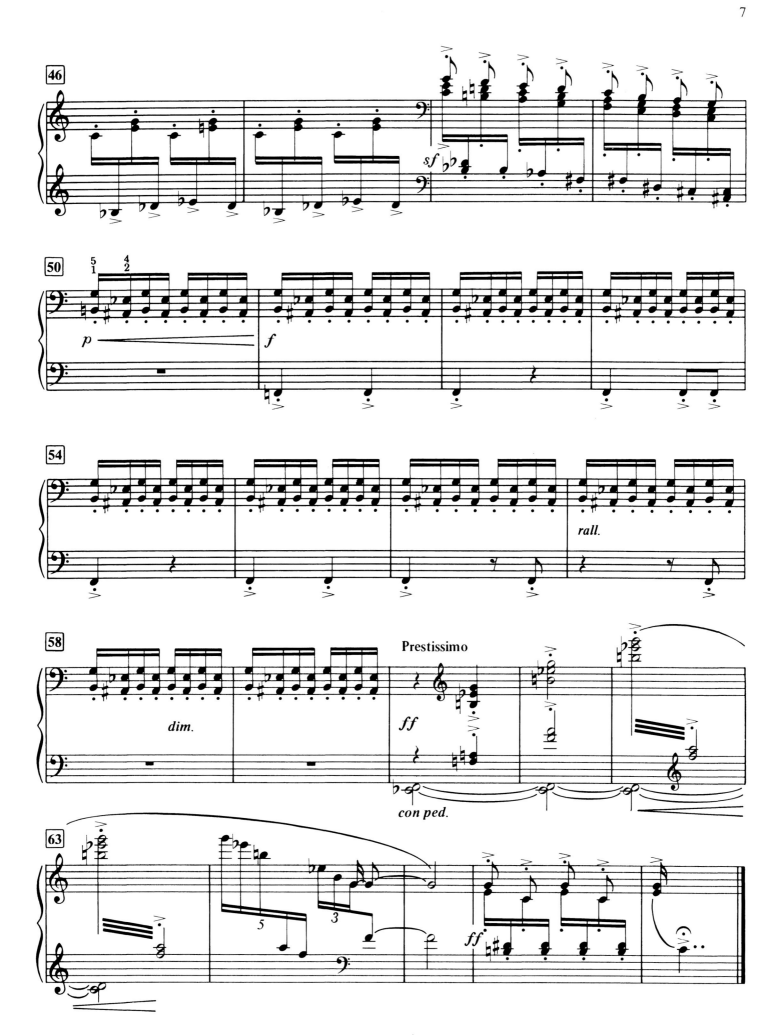

ALFRED MASTERWORK LIBRARY
Most Requested

Bach/18 Short Preludes
(Palmer)
Book (601)
CD (rec. K. O'Reilly) (16790)

Bach/Dances of J. S. Bach (Hinson) (600)

Bach/French Suites (Schneider) (700)

Bach/Two-Part Inventions (Palmer) (604)

**Bach/Inventions and Sinfonias
(Two- and Three-Part Inventions)** (Palmer)
Leather (4867)
Paper (Comb-bound) (606C)
CD (rec. Lloyd-Watts) (4056)

Bach/Selections from Anna Magdalena's Notebook
(Palmer)
Book (605)
CD (rec. Lloyd-Watts) (16792)

Bach/Well-Tempered Clavier, Volume 1
(Palmer) (2098C)

Beethoven/16 of His Easiest Piano Selections (383)

**Beethoven/13 of His Most Popular
Piano Selections** (390)

**Beethoven/Selected Intermediate to Early Advanced
Piano Sonata Movements** (Hinson)
Volume 1 (4841)
Volume 2 (4842)

Burgmüller/18 Characteristic Studies, Op. 109
(Hinson) (4829)

Burgmüller/25 Progressive Pieces, Op. 100 (Palmer)
Book (608)
CD (rec. Lloyd-Watts) (16787)

Chopin/14 of His Easiest Piano Selections (397)

**Chopin/19 of His Most Popular
Piano Selections** (389)

Chopin/Etudes, Complete (Palmer) (2500C)

Chopin/An Introduction to His Piano Works (Palmer)
Book (635)
CD (rec. Lloyd-Watts) (4013)

Chopin/Mazurkas (Palmer) (2481)

Chopin/Nocturnes (Palmer) (2482C)

Chopin/Polonaises, Complete (Palmer) (2480C)

Chopin/Preludes (Palmer) (610)

Chopin/Selected Favorites (Palmer) (611)

Chopin/Waltzes (Palmer) (2483)

Clementi/Six Sonatinas, Op. 36 (Palmer)
Book (609)
CD (rec. K. O'Reilly) (16771)

Czerny/30 New Studies in Technique, Op. 849
(Palmer) (591)

**Czerny/Practical Method for Beginners on
the Piano, Op. 599, Complete** (Palmer) (596)

**Czerny/The Art of Finger Dexterity,
Op. 740, Complete** (Palmer) (595C)

Czerny/The School of Velocity, Op. 299 (Palmer)
Book 1 (613)
Complete (612)

Czerny/The Young Pianist, Op. 823, Complete
(Palmer) (590)

Czerny/Selected Piano Studies, Volume 1
(Germer/Palmer) (597)

Debussy/Children's Corner Suite (Hinson) (667)

Debussy/Preludes, Book 1 (Hinson) (2594)

Debussy/Preludes, Book 2 (Hinson) (2598)

Debussy/Selected Favorites (Olson) (2495)

Hanon/The Virtuoso Pianist (Small)
Book 1 (617)
Book 2 (682)
Complete Edition (616C)
GM Disk, Book 1 (arr. Wren) (5715)

Hanon/Junior Hanon (Small) (518)

Köhler/Sonatina Album (Small)
Book (1710C)
Two CDs (rec. K. O'Reilly) (3997)

**Kuhlau/Nine Sonatinas, Opp. 20 and 55
for the Piano** (Palmer) (4889)

Mendelssohn/Songs without Words, Complete
(Hinson) (4860C)

Mozart/14 of His Easiest Pieces (384)

Mozart/21 of His Most Popular Pieces
(Palmer) (391)

**Mozart/Selected Intermediate to Early Advanced
Piano Sonata Movements** (Hinson) (4884)

Mozart/Six "Viennese" Sonatinas (Palmer) (1707)

Rachmaninoff/10 Preludes, Op. 23 (Baylor) (515)

Rachmaninoff/13 Preludes, Op. 32 (Baylor) (655)

Rachmaninoff/Selected Works (Baylor) (2423)

Satie/Gymnopédies and Gnossiennes (Baylor) (2501)

Schmitt/Preparatory Exercises, Op. 16 (Palmer) (1709)

Schubert/Impromptus, Op. 90 (Baylor) (544)

Schumann/Album for the Young, Op. 68 (Palmer)
Book (620)
Two CDs (rec. K. O'Reilly) (16796)

Schumann/Scenes from Childhood, Op. 15 (Palmer)
Book (632)
CD (rec. Lloyd-Watts) (16794)

Streabbog/12 Melodious Pieces, Book 1, Op. 63
(Palmer) (621)

Tchaikovsky/The Nutcracker Suite, Op. 71a (Hinson)
Duet, 1 Piano/4 Hands (4858)
Solo Piano (4856)
CD (rec. Reed/Reed) (16774)

Tchaikovsky/The Seasons, Op. 37b (Hinson) (4826)

Tchaikovsky/Album for the Young, Op. 39 (Novik) (485)

Tcherepnin/Bagatelles, Op. 5 (Olson) (551)

Villa-Lobos • O Polichinelo • Olson

Alfred

ISBN-10: 0-7390-0774-2
ISBN-13: 978-0-7390-0774-7

9 780739 007747

alfred.com